FERGUS
Comes to earth

Michaela Turner

BALBOA.
PRESS
A DIVISION OF HAY HOUSE

Balboa Press books may be ordered through booksellers or by contacting:

Balboa Press
A Division of Hay House
1663 Liberty Drive
Bloomington, IN 47403
www.balboapress.com.au
1 (877) 407-4847

Print information available on the last page.

ISBN: 978-1-4525-3072-7 (sc)
ISBN: 978-1-4525-3073-4 (e)

Balboa Press rev. date: 09/09/2015

To my two beautiful children, Katharine and Michael—you are more than I could have ever have dreamed you to be. I am so proud of everything you have been and everything you ever will be. Your patience, love, understanding, and selflessness when you were growing up allowed me to pursue my passion to help vulnerable children. You have the biggest and most generous hearts I know, and you act as a reminder to me every single day that angels are already walking on earth.

Foreword

I am a great believer in the connectedness of life and, even deeper, in the connectedness of all things through consciousness, or intelligence itself.

In *Is Your Life Mapped Out?* I wrote that we (as non-physical consciousness) exist infinitely in time and space, and as such we must exist before we are physically born on earth. Could this mean we could have a hand in selecting elements of the lives we live? I would say so. I believe we choose the where, the when, and the circumstances.

I enjoyed reading the story of Fergus because it plays into how I look at the world. It's a semi-magical story of a soul coming to earth and being taught by a wise soul (Abraham) before he incarnates. The book also has snippets of lessons about how we shape our lives, inspiration and insights that might help us overcome some of the challenges in our own lives.

I met Michaela Turner when she attended one of my workshops, and I could see very quickly that she was a creative, playful soul. I was not at all surprised when she told me she'd written *Fergus Comes to Earth*. I love that she has put ideas about consciousness and the nature of reality into an accessible story that anyone can read. The act of turning philosophical ideas into prose is a challenge Michaela has risen to, and I'm sure we will hear more about Fergus and his exploits as she continues the story in future books.

Dr. David R. Hamilton

Preface

Fergus Comes to Earth is a direct result of everything touched upon in this book. After working full time in an emotionally challenging environment, studying for seven years, and raising two children, there came a point where neither my mind nor my body could take any more. During all my work with children and families, I was always aware that there was a much easier way to help them work through the traumas that plagued them. Being oblivious to what I know now, my own personal life was a bit of a disaster, apart from the two important things in my life: my two children and my work. Unfortunately, as many of us know, it only takes one unbalanced area of our lives to upset and impact the others.

Becoming ill gave me the most wonderful opportunity (although I would never have said so at the time) to begin again. I was able to start piecing together who I *am* and regain my connection to the universe. It did not happen overnight, but the point was making the decision to get better. Once I had the knowledge from both a spiritual and a scientific perspective, I knew I would get better. I began to see the signs that were laid out in front of me, and as I followed them, I began to trust in the miraculous nature of the universe. Wayne Dyer is famous for saying, "When you change the way you look at things, the things you look at change" And boy, do they change!

I started to clearly hear my guides, who have been with me all the time. Although it might sound very spiritual to be hearing angels, I talk to them in a way I would speak to best friends—and what a sense of humour they have! I am the girl next door, another somebody whose life was turned upside down before reaching adulthood, the one who went on to make crazy decisions based on not knowing who I was. So when I say that if I can change my life, then you can, I mean it with every ounce of sincerity in my body.

Fergus Comes to Earth started from a dream, and the book came into being as a message from the angels. The book incorporates my own healing journey as Fergus's soon-to-be birth mother, with all that I could ever have hoped to write about. The surprise was that it took the form of a children's book, while speaking to adults in a way that will hopefully help their own healing journeys with simple messages for children to understand.

Fergus Comes to Earth is an introduction to a possible change in how we look at the way children are cared for within our education and care systems—that which is lacking in ensuring that all earth's children are cared for, to bring out the very best in each and every one of them and in humanity itself.

We have all the answers right inside of us to continue to live on this beautiful planet and bring a little heaven down to earth. I think each and every one of us deserves it. Don't you?

Acknowledgements

Fergus Comes to Earth has been a very special project for me. It is the first I have completed after losing my job with a children and families team due to chronic fatigue syndrome in 2009. Since then, there have been so many special people who have helped me, sometimes only with kind words and often without even knowing the impact they had on me at the time. It is said that by becoming grateful, you receive even more blessings in your life, and I can vouch for that. I would like to thank everyone whose lives have crossed mine in the last few years; you have all made becoming truly grateful one of the easiest things to do, including those who follow my Facebook page, Rainbow Keeper.

I would like to give special thanks:

To Jane Collingwood, a wonderful artist who sculpts the most incredibly lifelike babies, which sell worldwide. She found her talent whilst fiddling with some Blu-Tack when talking to a friend! Thank you so much for tracing the artist Ivan Gorda, knowing this was the one image that I'd fallen in love with, for the front cover for *Fergus Comes to Earth.* Thank you for the friendship and laughter you have brought back into my life.

To Ivan Gorda, of Komiskar Illustration, for giving me the permission to use his picture *Night Road* as the front cover for this book. I cannot thank you enough! I hope your art brings you everything that you could possibly hope for yourself, and more.

To my mother, Margaret Hempshell, who, after wondering where on earth her one and only child came from, has continued to be there for me despite all the worry that I have put her through over the many years. I love you, Mum.

To my daughter, Katharine Duffy, for her unwavering belief in me, and for even offering to help pay towards the publishing costs for the book.

To my son, Michael Duffy, who returned to the nest for a year and has had to put up with his dear mother talking to him about angels.

To Kay Noble, my friend who was there to bring out the inner craziness in me as if it was natural. She helped me bring all the wonder and magic back into my life on a daily basis. I have no doubt I will be working more closely with you in the near future, delivering workshops and talks. I know that every minute of it will be as much fun as it will be rewarding—just as life should be!

To David Hamilton for his brilliant work in showing how to integrate the science of how your mind affects your body and how to use this knowledge in your daily life. Your five-day workshop at Lendrick Lodge came to me not only at the right time but with the right information, giving me the confidence to get better. It brings me incredible joy and gratitude to read your beautiful comments in the foreword for this book.

To Mary Alvarado from Balboa Press. Just knowing you were there and would respond quickly to any questions made the whole process of writing and publishing my book so much easier.

Last but in no way least, to Michael Reynolds, who came back into my life the same week that Fergus was given to me by the angels. Not only have you been such a supportive friend, but I would have been lost without you for the proofreading, especially because even I could not always understand it on the first read through! By allowing me to use you as the father for Fergus, it made the writing of the story much easier. I am sure by the time you finally finished your role as proof reader, you actually felt like a father to Fergus, so thank you.

Chapter 1

In a faraway place, there are many young souls who are preparing to come to earth. Just like in our schools on earth, they have teachers and guides who are there to help prepare them for the lives ahead of them. Of course, how much preparation they receive often depends on the students' willingness to learn. The rewards for learning are very high: a lifetime to play and learn all about the magic of being human on a beautiful playground called earth.

All that the guides and teachers can do is hope that their students learn enough about the promise of the magic that being on earth has to offer. They know that most of their students will become distracted by all the exciting adventures, which may take them off of their true paths. If only they could remember all the lessons, then everything would be all right.

However, life on earth is not like that. Once their souls graduate and they are born on earth, they mostly forget everything they were taught. They are so busy learning the new skills of being a human that they don't have time to remember anything that would have helped them.

They are then alone with their new parents, missing all of the guidance and protection that their own homes had to offer. This is one reason babies cry all the time: they can never be sure of what is going to happen next. All they are able to see are blurred things in front of them, speaking a language they do not understand. They feel scared and alone, and their only chance is to fight for survival and return home as soon as possible.

The very early years of being on earth are really important. This is where new babies find out whether they have parents who can love them and understand their every need. Babies already know what they like and what they do not like, so they have to help their parents find this out too. Some children may have more difficult lives than other children, but it does not mean their parents love them any less. It is only because their parents have not yet remembered how truly magical they are, and they find it more difficult to help their own children.

There are many souls who are being taught much more in preparation for them to come down to earth so that they can remember who they really are as soon as possible.

Abraham, like most guides and teachers, is an older soul who rarely shows himself to the people living on earth. The guides are usually there, but people do not see or hear them. They do leave signs to help, but humans have not yet learned how to use all of their sight yet.

The guides may feel helpless and frustrated that their children don't notice the help being offered to them. All the questions that people ask are always answered—if only they knew it. The answers may be found in music that sings to their souls, in a passage of a book, or in a conversation with a friend or a stranger. The guides are always there, waiting for people to remember that the help they are looking for is right there inside of them or in front of them.

The guides do not get angry; they are very patient, hoping that their children will learn how to see or hear their guidance and follow the signs that they leave for them. All the guides know that life on earth can be a very harsh and scary place if people are not able to find their ways in life and they become very unhappy.

Chapter 2

Fergus is one of many special souls who will be very sensitive when they return to earth. This means these souls will easily pick up the thoughts and energy from other people. Not only may they think that these are their own thoughts, but they may even pick up on the physical pain from others too. These souls are called empaths.

There have been many born to earth before this time, and more have been remembering their gifts. All people in the universe have these gifts; they simply need to remember how to use them. Many empaths go on to become healers because they can understand other people's pain and are often the best people to help. Everybody has his or her own gifts. Sometimes souls come down to learn, and they may travel, paint, or sing; all these activities create magic for others. In the end they go on to share their gifts. It is what gives people the most pleasure, and when they help others in any way, their bodies respond and they also receive healing.

However, when young children are learning about their empath natures, it can be a very hard and confusing time. They have no idea what is going on around them. Not only do they have all their own thoughts and feelings, but also they are unaware that many of the thoughts are not really their own. They need to be taught this from an early age. If they don't know what is causing their pain, their bodies can be affected negatively, or they may act out of control and naughty. This is simply because they feel confused by everything they are feeling every day.

Fergus and other children still have to learn all of this. Until that time, they may feel anxious and uneasy in their surroundings, especially when they have to leave the safety of their homes or families. They may not know how to act, what to say, or what to do in many situations, making their bodies feel even worse. They may start to sweat, their tummies may feel wobbly, and they may be too afraid to talk because their words could come out mixed up. Life on earth can be very scary for many children.

This is not something a doctor can fix, but it does affect the body. That is why, on earth, they have special doctors who help everyone when they do not feel well. Where Fergus comes from, this is not a problem, because nobody ever gets sick; they don't feel pain, because they do not yet have physical bodies.

What Fergus does not know at this time is that he is one of many souls who will be able to remember most of this from a very young age. Before his time, over thousands of years, many like him have gone down. At first these people lived off the land and in harmony with nature, but life on earth began to change. As humankind discovered more and more, people became so busy and wanted more things. In the end the *things* became more important to them than anything else. That was when the teachings were lost.

What was once celebrated in life began to disappear. Spirituality became known as religion. Many stopped believing because the stories they were told did not make sense. Not only was the meaning lost; the entire true way for people to treat one another was forgotten.

Fergus will have a very special task during his time on earth, and so a very experienced guide looks after him. Abraham has been called to mentor Fergus to the best of his ability, but only as far as guiding him. That is all that he is allowed to do. He can only give him information to help Fergus with his life on earth. All souls have free will, and when Fergus is old enough, he will be left to make his own choices.

As an elderly, very wise guide, Abraham is dressed in an all-white suit with a black tie and black shoes. He looks elegant. He is tall and slim with silver hair and a moustache, as well as sparkling blue eyes that look like there are diamonds dancing in them. He can look like anyone; his appearance does not really matter and is only to give the impression of a senior teacher to those souls who are heading back down to earth.

Abraham knows that the task in front of him is serious. He knows the importance of the task that Fergus is destined to fulfil. It makes him shudder to think of what could happen if Fergus fails to complete his mission. Everything depends on Fergus and other souls being given the love and support they need to wake up and remember their gifts while they are young.

When babies are born on earth to be with new parents, they will often lie down and close their eyes to sleep. This gives their brains the time to be able to make sense of what they have seen and heard during the day. They do this so their bodies can have the best possible chance to grow and repair themselves, while their souls gets messages sent to them in the forms of dreams. At other times their eyes will be open, and the babies will cry for food, drink, comfort, or love. People believe that when their babies' eyes are open, they are awake, but that is not really true. They are not yet fully aware and don't understand the world around them.

These new children being born to earth only need to follow what makes them feel good; they should listen carefully to the advice they are given. This will help them find their way and keep on the paths to their final destinations without the distractions that are often in their way. Everyone has an inner knowing of what is right; one need only believe in oneself. There is not just one path, because everyone's path is different. The hardest part for the new children will be staying on their own paths. They will not be alone though, because they will soon meet friends along the way. Once they have served their purposes on earth or at their chosen time, they will leave their bodies and return home, into the vastness of space called the universe.

On earth, many people call this heaven. It is thought of as a place where men, women, children, and animals go when their souls leave their bodies. It is a place of great beauty, peace, and unconditional love. Any illness will be healed there, and newcomers are welcomed by all the people they have loved in the past. All this is true, but it is also mostly true on earth. It is almost exactly how people describe heaven. Nature is so incredibly beautiful, and so is every person on earth, in his or her own way. When people's hearts are filled with gratitude, they are so thankful for every day that they are alive, and they can really see all the magic around them. When a soul leaves its body, all it is doing is getting ready to come back to earth at another time and place.

From the time of Fergus's birth, Abraham can no longer help his young student or any of the other souls who are under his care. That is why Abraham has to help Fergus in any way he can, by trying to show him signs that will light the path for him to return home once he has completed his task and lived a well-loved life on earth.

In order for Abraham to guide his student to wake up and remember who he is, he has asked for the help of a most beautiful, gentle, and powerful angel, the queen of angels herself: Mother Mary. Mary radiates the presence of such emotional and motherly love. She keeps an overview of all that will happen from now until Fergus is ready to return home and be born again. Of course Mary is not the only angel who has this duty, but Mary's beautiful nurturing nature is called for now more than ever. Her role is ensuring that the young souls returning to earth now should not encounter too much emotional harm. This hurt may harden their hearts, leaving room for fear to enter and grow. This would be very bad because it would delay Fergus and all the other souls from remembering who they are; all they would have the energy for, would be surviving on earth, which would be very difficult. If that happens, Fergus and all of his friends will fail in their mission to help save humanity and also their mother, the earth.

There will of course be lots of other angels, fairies, and guides who will be waiting to be asked for help. These beautiful beings can only step in if they are asked to, or where someone's life is in danger but it is not that person's time to return home just yet.

Mary will keep a motherly eye on everything once Fergus is born, and that will include his parents, whom he has yet to choose. In fact, Mary is one of the keepers of the book of plans, where all souls make their contract before coming back down to earth before their next journey begins.

Like Abraham, Mary hopes that Fergus will consider his choice of parents carefully. They are aware of his building excitement and hope that he does not make his choice too quickly.

Fergus likes puzzles, and so there is always a chance he might choose a more difficult path, slowing him down or even stopping the chance he has of remembering why he is there. They hope that Fergus will choose at least one parent who is already under the love and guidance of an angel. An angel who works with people who have a special purpose: to pass on their gifts to help children. An angel is already watching over a particular lady who would make a good mother for Fergus.

Even if two people have yet not come together in a relationship or have not even met, the angel is already helping and guiding these two people together.

Chapter 3

Kate was born as an only child to parents who'd had very busy working lives. Kate had no brothers or sisters, and so she was very much alone for so much of her childhood. Her mum and dad ran their own businesses and kept moving around from town to town.

The only time that Kate was not alone was for the six months when Kate's mum and dad arranged to move to Majorca with another family. The other couple had three children, two girls and a younger boy. Those six months were the best time of Kate's childhood, and she had been really happy. She was no longer on her own, and that was when she developed her love for all animals and marine life. Next door to the apartments where Kate and her new friends lived, there was a marine park that had just opened, and they went there for her ninth birthday. Marine Land became a regular playground for the children, but watching the dolphins had been Kate's favourite thing to do, and she'd imagined swimming with them in the warm, wild ocean.

But most important for Kate was that she was no longer alone. Kate had a habit from a very young age to search among people for a special connection; she believed that there was someone from her life who was missing. Kate had always longed for a brother of her own, and so it was naturally boys to whom she was drawn.

When Kate had to return to England, the searching began again. Kate was never really conscious of this. That is to say, it was not in the front of her mind all the time, and she didn't know that much of her behaviour came from these feelings.

Unconscious thoughts can be sneaky and can creep in and out of our minds before we have time to recognise them. They are not at all like the thoughts where you are thinking about getting up and going outside to play or starting a job that needs to be done. Many unconscious thoughts come out in dreams; sometimes it's when our eyes are open and we are daydreaming, and sometimes it's when we sleep. Dreaming was one of the things that kept Kate company when she was on her own. These were her favourite times because when she was alone with her thoughts, she could create her own dream world.

Upon the return to England, one of the many dreams that Kate regularly had was of running around a big attic in excitement, uncovering beautiful pieces of furniture. Sometimes she would discover a whole room filled with beauty she had never seen before.

Kate loved these dreams, and it was how she learned to change things in her dreams. If there was something there that didn't seem special, she would change it, making it into something beautiful.

Kate liked where she lived after her return from Majorca. It was a lovely Yorkshire town, with a river and woods running behind her house. She would take herself and her dog to the river and play for hours. Kate eventually made friends, and they would play at the riverbank, sliding down on their backs. As they went, all they could smell was the waft of wild garlic, which overpowered their senses.

By this time Kate was dreaming more and more about having a brother, and she even asked her parents if they would adopt a boy. Kate felt so at ease with boys that she had even requested a football and a pair of boys' pyjamas for her birthday one year. In fact, she would have wished to become a boy, if she'd had the chance. However, Kate was happy with being a tomboy. In the winter months Kate would spend more and more time indoors, alone. Kate's parents, Richard and Joan, would be downstairs working in the restaurant they owned.

When Kate was not daydreaming, she could usually be found reading or watching television. With all the reading that Kate did, her vocabulary should have been very good, but she did not read books to learn. Kate read books in which she could lose herself, becoming part of the story to pass the time she had with only herself as company.

Kate would often visit her Nanna Teddy during the holidays. Nanna lived near the centre of Leeds, where Kate had first lived before moving to Majorca. Kate used to love returning there, feeling a sense of belonging with the big city close at hand. There was a large park with lots of trees right behind the house where Nanna lived. A large fair used to return several times a year, and she loved to watch the coloured lights in the dark as the rides swung around. It was here that she learned to love one ride the most: the Waltzers. Her aunt and uncle had taken her on it when she was five years old, and she had been scared to death. But as she grew older, she enjoyed it more.

At the back of the house, there was a big green park and a magical woods where she used to play. A lovely little stream ran through the woods, and there was a small pond filled with little fish. Kate would be lost in her own world, fishing with a net for sticklebacks or roaming around the woods and exploring with the dogs. It didn't matter what the weather was like; even if it was raining, Kate would splash through the puddles, dreaming her life away.

Kate would spend hours with Nanna baking, learning to cook, or reading. They would read different books, but it would lead to conversations on many subjects. It was during Kate's early years when she learned about Doris Stokes, a medium who could hear spirits and would relay messages to their loved ones. It was also at this time when she and Nanna talked about hands-on healing, which Kate intuitively knew she could do. That was when she heard for the first time about Kathleen, her great aunt who was no longer alive.

Kathleen was one of Nanna's sisters who had withdrawn from most of the world and had chosen to live in a tiny cottage in the middle of the woods. Kathleen was said to have had a beautiful way with children and animals. Nanna knew that Kate and Kathleen would have loved each other deeply, and she must have wondered if her sister's free spirit had been passed down to Kate. Maybe Nanna had already spotted the free spirit in her granddaughter.

Nanna worried that Kate would end up alone, just like Kathleen and herself. She was the first of many of Kate's teachers along her path to help wake her up to the treasures on earth. But as Nanna knew, it was not that easy! She said many times, "I wish I could put an old head onto your young shoulders!"

Chapter 4

Fergus had no physical body; his soul existed within what looked like a swirling mass of coloured energy. However, he had no trouble being a dedicated student and he was always very excited. Time did not really exist within the universe, so once Fergus finished his studies under his newly appointed guide, he was ready to go. The main tasks he had to complete were choosing his birth parents and writing his future.

Fergus was an excitable and inquisitive soul; he had even begun wondering what he would look like in his physical body. Fergus knew his thoughts were very powerful, and he had no reason to doubt that if he had a thought, it would happen, because everything was connected.

The universe lacked nothing, for all would be given when people emanated love. It was the language of the universe's life force, which flowed through everything. This was why it was so important that Fergus did not encounter any harm to his physical, mental, and emotional bodies.

Fergus also knew to only have positive thoughts if he wanted good things to happen. When fear or any sort of pain enters children's hearts, they start to lose the connection to the universe and then themselves. This is very sad because when this happens, they are always disappointed, and then their whole worlds become reflections of their disappointment. Wherever they look, there will be pain, suffering, hate, and cruelty. People soon become anxious and depressed after having lost their connection to the universe.

Somehow Fergus was drawn to Scotland. He did not know why, but he did know that he loved the mountains, the greenery, the lochs, the wildlife, and the trees. Oh, how he loved trees. He thought if he could chose somewhere magical, then this would help him remember who he was, and he would remember his mission.

Fergus caught himself imagining himself as a little boy with red hair, a hair colour which was common in Scotland. Children with red hair seemed so special: they were often childlike with a crazy sense of humour, which appealed to Fergus very much. He knew that children with red hair were often teased and made to feel self-conscious but that didn't bother Fergus at all.

However, Fergus was more excited about choosing his parents. He knew they would be the most important people in his life and would make such a difference to his success by trying to keep him on the right path. Of course they would not know exactly what it was he would have to do, but they would know what he was interested in and what he was good at, and they would help him by giving him the right experiences.

His biggest clues would be found if he followed what made him feel good—the things he enjoyed doing or things that made his heart sing. It came down to following his love, and that was all he needed to remember.

All this thinking made him feel even more excited. He had no doubts he would love his parents very much. He was such a sensitive soul filled with love that he would swell with pride when he thought of his new parents. He would glow with happiness, smiling all the time.

He only hoped that his parents would be able to help him, because if neither of his parents remembered who they were, it would make things much more difficult. Fergus knew he was going to have to make the right choice. What Fergus still had to learn was that all souls chose the right parents, because they chose them in order to learn something that would eventually let them help other people.

When people are happy and loving life, it is very rare that they will want to do anything else but return the help for everything that they have received. Over the years, people have started to gradually wake up on earth. It appears that for every decade that goes by, children are remembering their missions earlier and earlier. This has been their destiny, preparing for a new era of humanity. There will be more and more children and adults who will be ready to support the changes that need to take place on earth.

It can be frustrating for many children who have woken up or have come down to earth awake already, because they cannot understand human behaviour. They find people who worry about everyday things slightly odd because those people can't see that the only problems they have are the problems they created themselves. They haven't yet learned to watch their thoughts, and when they think bad thoughts about something, they keep attracting more problems. It is a circle that they can't break out of, and they end up creating a sickness in their bodies. Indeed, human beings are a very peculiar race. Who on earth deliberately wants bad things in life when there is so much good? People's guides and angels can only look on with a careful eye, willing them to see the signs and reminders they are putting in their pathways.

Some children can be very hurtful to other children, and they don't see that this is wrong. They can't see this at the time, because they only know what their parents, television, computer games, and everything that goes on around them have showed them. If a child is filled with fear, he or she can only pass on fear to others. If this fear is not released, the child will either go on to be horrible to others or be scared of others—or both.

Some of this is now being taught in schools to help children, but what teachers should be doing is helping their students learn to find what it is they love. When they have done this, they can teach them about what they will need in order to keep the love in their lives. They could love to learn about different countries and cultures, or climate. Perhaps they would love learning mathematics, or they might love languages such as English so that they can read and write to effectively communicate. But more important, they need to be told all the time how special they are. They need to be told that they are beautiful, because all souls are beautiful, with so many gifts that they can share and love.

The saying "Sticks and stones may break my bones, but words will never hurt me" is very wrong. Words that make us feel bad on the inside can stop us from ever waking up to the miracle that is inside each and every one of us. Words can wound the hearts of sensitive souls, and they sometimes feel that they want to curl up and hide. They start to cut off the love from their hearts and replace it with fear. Without a lot of support from family and friends, some children may feel that they are victims as they have this experience. Again, this is such a horrible situation because they are going to attract even more feelings of being unloved.

When bones break, at least the body has time to rest, and the quiet of the soul can be heard. This is also the time to learn new things that children might not have had the chance to before. But when the heart is hurt, it is really difficult for these children because no matter how much others may show them love or try to help them, victims can only see what they have been taught to see: that people will hurt them. They will not be able to change this until they can change their thoughts.

Chapter 5

Kate was easy to please as a child, and although she was able to keep some of the love in her heart as she grew up, she also had a lot of fear in her heart too. Kate's parents were arguing more and more, and she had no idea what she wanted to do with the rest of her life. At fifteen, she felt the pressure to decide which career she should follow. Kate had a very quick mind and a tongue that matched; she loved looking at information and analysing it. However, this did not show in school.

Only two jobs really caught Kate's interest. The first was becoming a doctor, because she could listen to the symptoms and work out what was wrong. Becoming a doctor was definitely going to be out of the question because she had no qualifications. She considered nursing, but Kate felt sure that she wouldn't be able to listen and remember the instructions being passed to her. Kate seemed to have difficulty with this; it never occurred to her that it was because she spent so much time in her own dream world.

Kate also thought of becoming a lawyer because she liked the idea of taking some information and arguing for a cause. This was where Kate's Nanna came in. Nanna was always helpful, often discussing the plight of others who were in need of help. When images of starving children would appear on the television, Kate became very upset and did not understand why no one was helping them, but they seemed too far away for her to help. She later discovered throughout her own life that not all children had someone to turn to when they needed help.

There are many reasons for this. Some children may be scared that they will not be believed, or they think their parents are too busy. Some may not want to upset their families. Even more upsetting is that some children believe that they have already told an adult, but they did not have the right words for the adult to understand. This leaves the poor child feeling like there is no help, and the child may never tell anyone again, at least until much later in life.

Being human was not very easy at times, and there was only one solution, but Kate would not find this out for years to come.

Chapter 6

Today was the first day that Fergus would meet his new guide and begin his learning. Fergus's energy was vibrating so high that one could almost hear him singing aloud. He had nothing to prepare and simply had to show up.

Abraham was also eager to meet his new students. Never before had he had the task of passing on all his knowledge to new humans. This was an exciting time for Abraham, especially meeting young Fergus, because he was an eager young soul. When Abraham first saw Fergus, he quickly realised that he would have to calm down this young spirit. He could not keep his focus on him, because Fergus's energy swirled around uncontrollably.

His first words to Fergus were spoken in a manner that was soothing, but they held a note of authority that Fergus could not ignore. "Fergus, come closer. I cannot see you hovering around there; you are moving too quickly. Come here so I can see you." As Fergus moved closer to his new guide, he lowered his head shyly, looking up from under his eyelashes. He dazzled Abraham with the most beautiful twinkling blue eyes. Fergus had already taken on some of the features he had chosen for when he came down to earth.

As Fergus moved closer, Abraham commanded him to come even closer. "Before we get started with your mission and choosing your parents, I want to talk to you about what has been happening on earth." Fergus picked up a serious note in his guide's tone, which let Fergus know that things on earth might not be what he had been expecting.

Abraham began. "Humans have evolved to a point where they need to remember who they are—and fast! Originally when human beings were first sent to earth, many remembered their beginnings in life and continued on the path of love, compassion, and kindness. It was these principles that helped them understand the laws of the universe, living off the land and respecting all life, but slowly over time nearly all these teachings have been lost."

"As time went by, people changed, learning many new skills. Humankind soon started to have a love for power instead of the power of love. The earth is now being destroyed, and you will be joining many others who have a mission to save not only Mother Earth but humankind."

Fergus stared at Abraham with his eyes wide open, which were twinkling as if his heart was crying. He could not understand what he was hearing. All that Fergus could think to say was, "But why? How could this have happened?"

Abraham explained. "Man did not understand or follow nature as it was intended. Instead of cooperating with each other, they believed that there needed to be leaders, and these leaders would have the greater share of the world's wealth. They started to draw lines across the earth, dividing it up into nations and even fighting each other for more land and power." Abraham's voice grew sterner as he told Fergus more. "Men started to be ruled by their egos instead of their hearts. They no longer wanted an equal share—they wanted everyone else's too. The divisions got worse, with people fighting over more land and more power, differences in religion, the riches of the land, and even the colour of skin. They have forgotten that they are all one, not only with Mother Earth but with the entire universe."

"What is the ego?" asked Fergus, who was becoming scared and confused.

"The ego is what helps us survive in the world. When children are first born, the ego helps keep them safe by letting others know what they need. As people grow and learn more, the need for the ego should become less. But because people are not following nature, they feel alone and isolated, and so the ego remains strong within them. The only function the ego should have in adults is to act as a signal for any dangers. The ego feeds on fear and will entice people to stay in the ego so that it can stay strong."

Fergus had no idea how he would cope on earth, and he wondered how he was going to remember everything he needed to know. He knew it was very likely he would forget all his teachings when he was born, and this thought troubled him deeply.

"Fergus, all you have to remember is to keep the love in your heart so that there is no room for fear," said

Abraham. "When humans feel lost, they lose all sense of who they really are, and then they only hear the strong voice of the ego, which will lead them into all sorts of trouble. People think they are doing the right thing by following the strongest voice in their heads. They don't realise that if they can keep their minds quiet, they will hear the call from the universe. They may hear the soft and gentle messages from angels, guides, and gods, or they may connect directly to the universe itself. These things are always there, gently or sometimes strongly reminding people who they truly are."

By this time Fergus had had enough. "How can they not see who they really are? Humans have all the gifts that we have up here. How can they not see how beautiful and special they are?"

"Oh, Fergus," said Abraham, "they only see with the two eyes in their head. They only see what is in front of them instead of using their feelings. When they look in the mirror, they can only see their outer shells and are never satisfied with what they see. They do what they can to look good so that other people will not tease them. They don't know they should look inside, and even if they have been told, they simply don't know how to do so anymore."

Abraham became concerned about his small friend; he had forgotten that Fergus was a very sensitive soul, and he could see the pain in the boy's eyes. He realised that he had not yet said enough about the problems on earth, and he felt a wave of compassion come over him. He felt that it was now time to take on a more fatherly role. Abraham moved closer to Fergus and gently moved down to the level of his face, being careful not to stand over him and scare him. He knew that while Fergus was thinking of the sadness on earth, he might find Abraham's presence overpowering.

"Fergus," Abraham continued in a much gentler tone, "people have gone into battles and killed thousands of their own, fighting for control of their land or the land of others." Fergus could hear the compassion in his mentor's voice and longed to go even closer to Abraham, as if a secret was being passed between them. "My young friend, people have forgotten that they are all one, and that they are meant to help one another—not murder or steal." Fergus felt like crying and tried to stop his tears from coming. Abraham had not finished with his story. "People went on and built more and more destructive weapons to fight for what they wanted, but at the same time they were beginning to make luxuries, and they kept wanting more. They soon realised that the more things they made, the more people would want them—and the more money could be made. This was all right for a while, but as time went by, some people got more and more while others got less and less."

Fergus was even more upset by humankind's behaviour, especially as Abraham went on to tell him that the earth was now suffering. Fergus was very quick to ask, "If people are happy because they are getting what they want, why is the earth suffering?"

Abraham let out a long, deep, and sorrowful sigh. It was harder to explain than he had first thought. "You see, Fergus, along with all of the other souls who are to be born on earth around the same time as you, you will have to act quickly in order to turn humanity around and save the earth." He knew that Fergus was aware of all the beauty on earth, and to be a witness to the earth suffering was something that might be too hard for the boy. If he feels the pain too badly, he will not be able to return to a place of love and will be trapped in fear among so many other humans on earth.

Fergus wanted to know much more about what Abraham had to tell him, but the lesson was coming to an end so he had to choose his next questions carefully. Fergus wanted to know what humankind was doing to harm such a beautiful planet. Abraham continued to tell his young student how people had polluted the earth. "They now have so many inventions that people no longer keep things until they are broken; they buy new ones to replace the old because they like the new colour or they want a newer model. They throw the old ones away. Then there is all the packaging that they put everything in to sell the items. There is now so much waste that they don't know what to do with it. There are also companies that drill into the earth to find oil and gas even thought they know that it causes problems to the environment."

Abraham could see Fergus's energy becoming unstable as he shook with grief. Abraham decided to change the subject. "Have you given any thought to what you think you should be doing to help humanity while you are down on earth?"

Fergus looked a bit confused. He didn't feel that he had a choice in the matter; he thought the decision had been made for him. After hearing about the state of the world, he replied, "I will help people remember who they really are so that we can all help bring the earth back into her natural balance."

Abraham looked pleased. Fergus probably would never remember that he was told how poorly the earth was doing before being asked that question. Fergus's energy was still low when he left Abraham. However, Abraham was happy that his plan had gone well, and he could only hope that Fergus would start to focus his mind fully on his task and that his depression would lessen in time for their next lesson.

Chapter 7

There is one thing that remains constant, and that is change. Even the cells in our bodies are being replaced every day. Change also found its way to Kate's carefree childhood: her parents were separating.

It was April Fool's Day, and Kate took a phone call while she was at school. Her mother was going to collect her to tell her that she was leaving her father—and that Kate was to stay with her dad. Kate was devastated. Although she knew her mother would be leaving, she had never thought that her mum would not take her with her. Kate was just turning sixteen, but she felt like a small child, and she couldn't imagine her life without her mum around.

Kate was due to leave school and start working with a local hairdresser where her mum used to get her hair done. It was Joan, Kate's mum, who had helped Kate get a job there. Kate really liked the work and the other girls who worked there. She also worked downstairs in the pub, taking out meals and washing up. She enjoyed meeting new people.

The only down side was that Kate knew her father was really unhappy without her mum, and this made her feel sad. Kate saw her mum regularly, and she really liked her mum's new partner, Peter. He was very quiet, but Kate could tell that he was a nice, caring man. It was not long before her father met a new girlfriend, which seemed to make him happy for a while.

Kate made sure that she focused on all the good things in her life, but she could not help but worry more about her father. Sandra, her father's new girlfriend, brought more and more strangers into their home, and Kate knew that something was very wrong. She did not want to worry her mother or Nanna, so she kept her worries about all the arguments to herself. To make matters worse, someone told Kate that her father was now taking drugs.

Kate lived in a small village and knew nothing about drugs, only that they could be dangerous and were illegal. She also knew that they could make someone feel good for a short time, but then the person soon found it very hard to stop. She had no idea who to talk to about her father, which made her feel very anxious and frightened. It was around this time that Kate read in the newspapers about younger children who had been hurt by their parents, and instead of thinking about her own worries, she realised that things could be a lot worse for her. By now Kate had a strong feeling that she would be able to help other children because she understood how scared they must be.

Kate had been seeing John, her boyfriend, since she was seventeen. After about a year he asked her to move in with him, and she was delighted. They may not have moved in together so soon, but John knew how scary things were for her at home. Kate continued at work and saw very little of her dad, who by now had got into trouble with the police. It was a hard time for Kate, and she felt worried that people would think badly of her; her heart filled with fear and shame. Of course no one really thought badly of her—it was only in her mind.

When John asked Kate how she felt about moving to Scotland for a new job, she did not hesitate. Kate saw this as a new start.

Chapter 8

When Fergus was by himself after his first meeting with Abraham, he asked for help to understand what life on earth would really be like. He did receive help in the form of a vision, but it was very confusing. He had been hoping for something that would help him understand, but he did not know what his vision had meant.

Fergus knew that the best thing to do was to explain the vision to Abraham and ask him if he could help him understand what it all meant. Fergus once again looked forward to his next lesson and waited patiently for Abraham to arrive.

Abraham gave a sigh of relief when he saw that Fergus was looking brighter than when he had left him after the last lesson. It was also a good thing that Fergus was calmer and much less excitable. Abraham noticed that Fergus had a puzzled look on his face, but this was no surprise given what his young student had just seen. There were no secrets in the universe, and a guide like Abraham already knew the answers Fergus sought.

Abraham did not need to beckon Fergus to come closer on this occasion; the boy rushed eagerly to his side, keen to start explaining what he had seen.

Fergus told Abraham his vision from the beginning. He had seen a red-haired lady in her garden talking to her family. The lady's name in the dream was Kate. A friend of Kate's, Jane, also with red hair, called to see if she would like to go shopping. Jane had brought Murray along with her, who was Jane's boyfriend. Kate explained that she could only be away for couple of hours because she had plans later in the day to see her mum. The three of them headed off to the new shopping centre that Jane had wanted to visit. It was a brand new shopping centre, and despite Kate not liking shopping, she agreed to go.

As they walked along, Murray started to brush at his sleeve, and both women burst out laughing as they watched him. Murray had a condition called obsessive compulsive disorder, which he had been learning to control as well as he could. He felt no annoyance at all as the girls each grabbed one of his arms and skipped along on either side of him.

Fergus was about to continue with what he had seen, but Abraham was quick to stop him. "Fergus, before you go on, I think this is a good time to explain what you have seen so far. This way I can explain things to you as we go along, and hopefully I can help you to understand the meaning of what you have seen so that we do not miss anything."

"So what was I seeing when the man Murray was so worried about having dirt on him? It doesn't make any sense to me at all. What is wrong with dirt?" asked Fergus.

Abraham wondered how to explain what having compulsive behaviour was like for someone who suffered from them. "Well, it all stems from anxiety, so someone who suffers from a compulsive behaviour has lots of thoughts that he finds very hard to stop. He has feelings of being worried or even frightened, and the thoughts are very difficult to ignore. For some people it might mean they have to keep washing their hands to keep them clean after they have touched something, or it may be that they have to have belongings in a certain place, facing the way they like them. There is no real reason why they have the thoughts. They simply find it difficult to deal with them."

"So are you telling me that people on earth do not understand that thoughts are just thoughts and that they are not real?" Fergus asked.

"Exactly," replied Abraham. "People do not understand who they are, and so they think the thoughts they have *are* who they really are. This also means that if people have had something bad happen to them in their past, they think that their thoughts about it are real."

Fergus quickly interrupted. "But that is not true! They just had an experience that affected them at the time; it is not who they are. Why do people forget this?"

"Ah, Fergus, this is not explained to people. Their thoughts are so powerful, as you know, that they don't know that they can simply change their thoughts into something much nicer. But many people *do* know this, and they are the ones who go on to live healthier lives. The others think far too much about what has happened, and then the thoughts become part of them—or so they think. Many people are able to get help when they have had problems in their lives, and they are able to talk to someone to help them understand their thoughts better. If children were taught how amazing their bodies are and how special each child is, it would make a big difference to them."

Fergus was a very bright and inquisitive soul, and he was about to ask more questions, but Abraham knew that this was distracting Fergus from the real reason he was here, which was to find out what his vision had meant. Abraham urged Fergus to continue with his story.

Chapter 9

Kate loved the north of Scotland and the countryside. She loved that no one knew her there, she loved the fact that it was such a safe place to live, and she loved the thought of leaving the past behind her—or so she thought! Kate continued to work as a hairdresser for a while, but she could not shake off the feeling that she wanted to help children who needed help. Kate had left school with no qualifications, and so she had no idea how to chase her dream.

More time passed. Kate really did like living in Scotland, but she still did not have anyone to encourage her to go after her dreams, and so part of her still felt a little lost. Her relationship with John had broken down, and now she had to learn to look after herself.

Kate still spent a lot of time thinking about her life, which seemed hard, and she spent too much time worrying, which became a bad habit. Kate still had so much to learn, but she did not know this, and so she made the same mistakes again and again, not learning and not growing.

The problem was that Kate was tired all the time. She did not know her thoughts were making her so tired. Kate would sit and think some more and become even more tired.

Kate had to move when she separated from John, and she found herself in a new town, where she found some very good friends, Jane and Mike. Both of them lived nearby, and she saw them on most days. It was here where Kate learned to laugh once again, and she found her energy starting to rise.

Kate had told Jane and Mike that she wanted to work with children, and with their support she went back to school to study for the qualifications she needed in order to work with vulnerable children. She also started to do some volunteer work at a crèche and took a small, part-time job at a youth club for teenagers. Life was beginning to feel good, as she enjoyed her new work. After a year Kate went on to work in a children's home, which she loved. Mike had moved abroad, and she did not see Jane quite as much because she was busy working all the time.

Within a few years, Kate had finally made it to university, where she studied to become a social worker. Kate had also studied counselling, but in the end she chose social work. While Kate studied, she worked with children and families from residential schools and within the community.

Kate and Mike kept in touch for a few years, but eventually they lost all contact with each other. Kate by now had also lost contact with Jane too. Although she thought of them often, she was always busy working or studying. Time seemed to go by so quickly, and very shortly after becoming a social worker, Kate got a job specialising in protecting children. This meant even more studying.

All the time that Kate was busy working and studying, she had little time for meeting friends, and life again became hard. Kate had to take time off of work regularly due to illness, and it was because her mind was so tired. Eventually, like many others who worked in jobs that were very hard on their feelings, she found herself no longer being able to carry on. Kate saw a special doctor who helped people who had long-term tiredness, called chronic fatigue syndrome. It was two years before Kate had the energy to stay out of her bed for more than one hour at a time. She was left feeling very sorry for herself. She had lost her job that she had worked so hard for, but she had no choice but to put that behind her and try and get herself well again.

Chapter 10

Fergus continued to tell Abraham his vision. "As Kate, Jane, and Murray drew closer to the new shopping centre, their mouths dropped at the size of it. Never in their lives had they seen anything like it before. Kate felt a feeling of dread, hoping that Jane would not want to explore all of it."

"From a distance the shopping centre looked like one big giant play park. The only thing Kate could compare it to was pictures of Disney Land that she had seen on the television and in books. It certainly looked very grand and exciting. Jane and Murray yelped with joy when they saw the size of it, but Kate was worried about getting lost and decided to stay as close to Jane and Murray as she possibly could."

"The first thing the three of them did was climb into the first lift they saw and go to the top floor so Jane could look at art supplies. As they got into the lift and pressed the button to go up, a metal shutter came quickly down between them. Kate and Jane were at one side of the shutter, and Murray was left at the other side of the shutter. The side in which Kate and Jane found themselves quickly shot sideways to the left. Jane laughed with her crazy sense of adventure. Kate felt frightened and anxious, and she vowed to keep very close to Jane."

"The two ladies found themselves by a fairground ride. Jane quickly jumped on board, but Kate could not keep up with her and had to take a seat far away from her friend. This made Kate feel uneasy. The ride set off, quickly spinning around. Kate soon found herself relaxing as it began to move, spinning them all the way around as it went."

"Once the ride had finished, they set off to find Murray, whom they found buying Jane's birthday present. None of them gave the funny experience in the lift a second thought—that was, until Kate realised that she had left her bag in the ride. The three of them soon managed to find a nice gentleman who offered to help them find the bag. While he went off to search, he told them he would make sure the bag would be taken to the shop that sold jeans, because that was where Kate wanted to go. Normally Kate liked to buy her clothes out of charity shops; it was her way of helping the planet by recycling."

"Kate, Jane, and Murray set off to the jeans shop to pick up the lost bag. However, the shopping centre was so big that the first thing the three of them had to do was ask for directions. Kate felt a hint of fear after being told that they had to get into another lift. She had no choice but to get in and hope for the best."

"Kate could not believe her eyes when two doors shot open, almost sucking Jane out into a different direction. Kate and Murray looked at each other in shock as they got out of the lift on the other side once the doors had opened."

"This time Kate found herself with Murray in an amusement centre with all kinds of computer games, as well as stalls where they could win prizes. This time Murray darted off, leaving Kate no other choice but to follow."

Fergus finished telling Abraham about his vision, explaining how he could feel everything that Kate was feeling; he tried to wait patiently for his mentor to say something. Abraham waited for a few seconds, trying to think of the best way to explain his thoughts.

"Fergus," Abraham started, "I told you yesterday about the problems that the earth is facing. Well, your vision showed many of the distractions that you will be faced with while you are there."

"So earth really can be like a great, big playground with so much fun to be had?" Fergus asked.

Abraham explained that people on earth were meant to be happy and to enjoy their time on earth. He then went on to say, "Mostly, people on earth are not happy. They feel that there is so much more to life, but they don't know what it is. The experiences of the people in your vision are telling you that people have an inner knowing of what they want to do in life. There are so many distractions in the form of what people think of as real life. People have to work to pay for the homes they live in and to put food on the table, leaving them very little time for themselves, especially if they have children, partners, or parents to care for."

"The language that their elders taught them became just words, and often the true meanings were lost. It is only when they have time to be silent and are on their own that they have time to remember who they really are. The lady's lost bag search symbolises the search for herself. She could not find her way because of all the experiences she had to have first."

"Some people choose to have a harder time on earth in the earlier years so that they then can understand the real meaning of what their own lives mean. It also helps them know where they have to go and what they have to do next. This is a very special time for them because they can now see all the magic that has happened in their lives to make sure they end up in the very place they are standing right now, having become everything they were meant to become! Only the people who give up are unhappy because they think their stories are over, when in fact they have only just begun!"

Chapter 11

Kate very slowly started her journey to recovery, and she knew just how lucky she was to have so much help from a special friend who knew what it was to live with being tired all the time. She had also become very good at following any of the signs that seemed to appear to her at times; it felt like it was the only thing she was able to do. Kate was determined that she was going to get better, yet the doctors remained helpless, only being able to help her make the most of her life rather than get well again.

At times it felt that she was getting help from the angels, and one clue led to another. Kate had already learned Reiki, which is a form of hands-on healing. She had already suspected that she was getting help from above when she had helped some other people, but because she was so tired all the time, she'd forgotten everything she was starting to remember.

At first Kate made friends with a lady in the hospital, Susan, who had suggested that Kate visit Bisong, a

Chinese medical doctor nearby. Bisong also taught Qi Gong, which simply means "working with energy." Kate went to do some volunteer work with Bisong at the Shen Foundation to help pay for her some of her classes. It was here where she made another leap in her recovery. Susan had suggested several times that Kate should meet her friend Kay, believing that they may enjoy working together. Kate and Kay instantly liked each other, quickly became friends, and were able to help each other.

Through Kay, Kate met Angela, who was a Louise Hay life coach. Once again, Kate had found another friend who helped her look at her own thoughts more closely and focus only on the good thoughts. Kate and Angela then went on to train for five days with a wonderful teacher named Dr. David Hamilton, who taught them about how the mind really had power in healing the body.

It was during this time that she came to understand that if her thoughts had made her ill, then her thoughts could make her better again. But what she loved even more was that the science she learned from Dr. Hamilton backed up everything she had learned in Qi Gong from Bisong. One of the things that Kate now shared with everyone who wanted to help themselves was the wonder of tummy breathing. This helped unblock all the sad emotions that were stored in the tummy while giving all of the organs a lovely massage. The very best thing for Kate was that it helped her concentrate on her tummy, which stopped her from thinking. Kate still found it strange that not one person in her life before she became unwell had told her how tiring thinking could be. This is especially so if people have suffered in their lives before they learn to love themselves, because this leads people to say bad things to themselves. Kate often wondered why people were never taught to be kind to themselves.

When Kate began to feel grateful for all the help that she was receiving and for everything in her life, she received even more help. With Kate being so tired and still thinking in her head, she missed some very important messages from people, and it would take her two or three times before she started to pay attention. One of these messages was that she needed to work with her angels more. Kate knew she only had to ask them for help and be ready to hear their answers, which meant that Kate really had to quiet her mind to be able to hear her angels slowly guiding her along the new path laid out for her.

One of the best decisions Kate made during her recovery was getting a new furry friend, Sam. Sam was a very handsome German shepherd who was only ten months old when he first came to live with Kate. By then she and Sam lived in a beautiful coastal village called Rosemarkie, a town with a powerful source of energy from the Fairy Glen. The house where they lived was very close to a lovely beach where dolphins could be seen at the changing of the tides. There was also a beautiful walk in the woods with two waterfalls, and many believed a lot of fairies lived there. The village had a lovely little pub that appeared to sway like the leaning tower of Pisa, as well as a little shop that sold all-natural products and crystals. Kate would often go into the store, called Panacea, even if it was just to have a cup of tea with the lovely lady who looked after the shop. People would come to visit for holidays in Rosemarkie, and later they'd return to make a life for themselves there.

Kate met many new and wonderful friends by walking Sam in the village. She even met lots more people from a group called Highland Dogblog. These people loved their dogs so much that they even had birthday parties for them. Kate really did love where she lived, and with her beloved Sam by her side, she had everything she needed. What better way to learn the lessons of love, kindness, and compassion than through a helpless animal that only knew how to love her? Kate soon understood why people called dogs man's best friend, and a year later Sam had a new friend of his own: a black Labrador called Jenny came to live with them.

Kate's new world was becoming as magical as she believed it could be. She had spent a long time learning and practicing everything she had been taught. Then it happened—the moment when Kate knew for sure that she was receiving messages from her angels. She learned that she only had to ask her angels a question, and the answer would appear to her. Kate was the happiest that she had ever felt in her life. However, she had one fairly bossy angel in her life who would tell her to go do something different from what she had planned to do. He was definitely a male angel as he had a very strong masculine presence, but he was caring and compassionate and never pushed her beyond her limits, even telling her to rest when she needed it. Nevertheless, he pushed Kate, and Kate did not speak to him how she thought she ever should speak to an angel; in fact, she would answer him back and be cheeky to him. Regardless, her love and trust in him grew more and more each day.

Kate still had problems with being tired so much of the time, but she also found out that she was very sensitive to the energy of the sun, the moon, and the earth. She accepted her tiredness now as part of who she was. One thing that Kate had learned from her good friend Kay was the law of attraction. Kay had been teaching this for years. Kate never asked for anything for herself, but she had found herself thinking more and more about her old friends Jane and Mike.

Chapter 12

Fergus continued to tell Abraham his vision. "Jane had found her way to the exact shop that she was looking for, an art shop, so that Jane could buy new supplies for her work. In fact, she had been enjoying looking at everything so much that she hadn't noticed how long she had been separated from Kate and Murray. Jane headed off to find them. The three of them set off once again to try to get Kate's bag back. Then all of a sudden Jane got a phone call to go collect her son from school, because he had come down with a fever. Jane managed to find her way around the great big shopping centre without a problem, and she found the right exit to go home. Kate and Murray continued on their journey to find the shop where Kate's bag was waiting for her."

"The two of them walked around aimlessly, trying to find the shop without having to get into another lift. They got as close as they could, but eventually they needed to ask for directions. Thankfully they were told that they were on the right floor and did not need to take another lift, much to Kate's relief. As they hurried along, something caught Kate's eye. She yelled at Murray to wait and then ran inside into a crèche where parents left their children while they shopped. Kate had always wanted to work with children, and Murray soon noticed the sign in the window that said they were looking for people to work there. Murray waited for Kate outside."

"All of Kate's worries appeared to vanish into thin air. As she ran up to the first group of children she came upon, she dropped on her knees and joined in with all the fun and games they were having. The children loved Kate because she listened carefully to what they were saying, letting them take the lead in the play, and joined in when it was her turn. The children seemed so excited to be sharing their game with her that she was able to keep them interested in what they were doing."

"By the time the lady in charge of the crèche walked over to Kate, she had realised what a wonderful and natural way Kate had with the children. Kate asked her about working there, and it was agreed that she would start the following Monday for a trial period."

"Kate left the crèche and found Murray waiting outside for her. He hadn't wanted to interrupt her because he knew that Jane would tell him off. It was the first time Kate had been so happy in a long time, and Murray was mesmerised by the change he saw in Kate while she played with the children."

"Murray welcomed Kate, who had a big smile on her face, and then asked her if she was ready to go find her bag. Kate looked at Murray, shrugged her shoulders, and replied that they were ready to leave; she no longer needed the bag that they had been hunting for. Murray grinned at Kate and was excited to tell Jane what had happened. He knew Jane would be delighted that her friend had found what she had been looking for all along."

Fergus breathed a long sigh, pleased that he had finished his story. "That is the end of what I saw, Abraham. Please tell me what the end of the dream means," he begged.

"Well, Fergus, you saw Jane receiving an important phone call from the school telling her that her son was unwell. She did not even think about how she was going to get out of the shopping centre; she was not worried about getting lost. She only had one thing in mind, and that was getting to her child. Jane did not worry about it, and so she was able to go straight to the exit without getting lost because she had no fear of doing so. Jane knew what she was doing and went straight to the school with no distractions or diversions."

Fergus jumped in. "Jane had no fear, so she was able to go straight to the exit."

"That is true, Fergus. Just like life, when a person has no fear, they seldom get lost."

"Kate had been searching for her bag for such a long time, and it was her own fear that stopped her from getting to where she wanted to go." Fergus let out a huge squeal and laughed. Kate had been so busy looking for her bag that she nearly missed what was under her nose: the chance to work with children."

"This is often the way things are, dear Fergus. People have their minds set on one thing, and this is why we often try to help people by showing them something even better. When Kate found the crèche, she realised that she did not really care about her bag; after all, it was only an empty shopping bag. Often when people are unhappy with their lives, they feel that something is missing. The missing piece is often themselves."

"Is this when they start to see the beauty in the world?" asked Fergus.

"Yes, this is so," replied Abraham. "There may be trouble on earth, but it's nothing that can't be mended. When people start to realise that there is so much magic in the world and how beautiful the earth really is, then more and more people will want to protect the earth as they would their own children. It is happening already, Fergus. You will not be alone when you are down there; there are so many adults, young people, and children ready to make the earth green once again."

There was only one thing that Fergus wanted to ask now. "So who is Kate? Why did she turn up in my vision?"

Abraham gave a great big roar and could hardly stop himself from laughing out loud. "Fergus, child, Kate is your mother."

Fergus did not know whether he should feel happy or cross about this. What had happened to his choice? He had not chosen this lady to be his mother! Choosing his parents had been something he had been really looking forward to doing. He asked in a very small voice, "What happened to my choice? I thought I got to choose my parents."

Abraham continued to laugh. "But you already have, Fergus. She came to you in your vision. Remember: there are no secrets in the universe. You could spend eternity looking for your parents, but like everything, it all comes to you. Your souls must have made a match. Tell me, Fergus, had you given any thoughts to what your parents would be like? Had you thought about where you wanted to go once you were back down on earth?"

Fergus started to feel a bit silly because of course he had, right down to one of his parents having red hair and living somewhere magical in Scotland.

"If it makes you feel better, Fergus, Kate is an excellent choice for your mother."

"But," stammered Fergus, "my mum is filled with fear. How could she be a good mother to me? How can she help me when she does not know who she is yet?" Fergus was confused and wanted an answer. How was this lady going to be the perfect mother for him?

"Fergus, remember—that was just one piece of the puzzle that you saw. In your vision, Kate had found her joy in caring for children, but her work took her much further than that. What you do not know is that your mum became unwell, and while she was ill, she took the chance to find out who she really was. Think about it: she had to lose her old life, leaving a blank canvas to create her new life."

oul

Chapter 13

Fergus thought some more about his new mother. Although he did not feel certain that Kate would be the right mother for him, he had noticed her red hair and freckles, which tickled him. He knew that all he had to do was trust that everything would be all right, and it would be.

This led Fergus's imagination to start running wild again. He thought of being brought up in Scotland, surrounded by trees and water. He thought about how his mother would help him remember who he was. He really did have more faith after Abraham told him that Kate had found out who she really was.

There was only one thing missing. He knew who his mother was going to be, but what about his father? Fergus was ready to find out more.

Of course Abraham knew exactly what his young student was going to ask him, and he was ready for him. He knew that Fergus still had unanswered questions, but Abraham knew that with his help, Fergus would be soon ready to leave his home and be born into a physical body on earth.

Abraham decided to beat Fergus to his questions and show him exactly who his father was and how both his parents came together. When Fergus showed up, Abraham said to him, "Come here. You have questions about your father. I want to show you how special both your parents are and why they are perfect to raise you."

Fergus was over the moon with joy, but nothing prepared him for what he was about to see. The first thing he saw was Kate as he had seen her in his own vision, so she must have been much younger in the vision than she was now. Next to her was a fairly tall man with unusual coloured eyes. Fergus could not make out if they were brown or green, but they appeared to be a very soft light brown in colour, and his parents laughed so much. He also saw them console each other through difficult times. His father's name was Mike. He caught a glimpse of his father's Celtic origins, making him jump with joy. He saw that his parents were only friends, yet the love between them was very obvious. Then the vision stopped.

"Wait!" shouted Fergus. "Where has he gone? Why are they not together? I thought I was going to see my father. Is he not my father?"

Abraham went on to tell Fergus that Mike already knew who he was at that time, but he had to wait for Kate to find herself as well. "If they had gotten together at that point, although your father may have helped your mother wake up, they would not be the same people they are now."

The next thing Fergus saw made him giggle. If he had any doubts about the help that the guides and angels could offer on earth, he had none now.

Mike and Kate had lost touch with one another. That was the one thing that they had tried very hard not to do, but sometimes things happened and people drifted apart. By now Mike was living in another country. Both of them had been searching for each other for years. Mike had tried contacting Kate with the telephone number he had over the years, and every time all he heard was a continuous tone, indicating that there was no such number anymore. Mike was no longer able to reach her.

Years passed quickly, and then Kate no longer wanted a mate. She was so happy being single, living alone, and enjoying her new life. Kate's work was as important to her now as it had been before she became ill; it was simply different work than what she'd dreamed of doing. Kate had a dream one night that changed all of that.

Kate found herself on a windowsill that was just like the one she had seen in the film *Peter Pan*. In front of her stood a slim man, but she could not see any of his features. Behind her was a young boy. Kate was unsure about what was happening; she only knew that the man did not want to take her with them. The boy grabbed hold of her hand, and away they went, flying through the night sky. Kate had never felt such freedom. There was no fear in her, only excitement, and she enjoyed every minute of flying with her new friends.

Kate could not believe all the magic she saw, but the one thing that stood out more than anything was the bright, vivid colours. They flew past small cottages that she had only ever seen in films such as *The Lord of the Rings* and *The Hobbit*. The doors had been painted with bright, happy colours. When the three of them arrived where they were going, the man from the dream introduced Kate to everyone there. The people in the dream did not appear to have any clear features, only a vibrating white energy. Kate had never felt such love, kindness, and compassion. She had never seen or felt anything so beautiful in her whole life.

While still dreaming, Kate was then back in her bed at home. She didn't want to wake up, because she was sad to think this beautiful memory was only a dream. When she opened her eyes, sitting next to her on the bed was the man from the dream. He handed her a bag of sweets, and in the bag the sweets were the shapes of things she had seen in her dream. The man had done this to let her know that everything she had seen was indeed real. Kate also knew that the man in her dream was her soul mate.

Kate awoke from her dream and was surrounded by the loving energy she had felt in her dream. The energy was so powerful, beautiful, and loving that she stayed as still as she possibly could, for as long as she could, before going back to sleep.

Kate had not believed that soul mates existed, but she was now unsure. Kate had instantly realised that she had a special connection with Susan, with Kay, and with Jane. Jane now lived in the village next to Kate. Kate had already questioned whether the three ladies in her life were part of one soul family; maybe there was a soul mate waiting for her to find him.

Kate's search had begun once more, but this time she knew exactly who she was and what she wanted. There were many signs for Kate to follow, and she did, questioning everything. Kate did not go out looking for signs, because she was busy creating a new life, but she knew them when she saw or heard the messages that other people had for her.

At the same time that Kate had the dream, Mike, who was constantly disappointed with not being able to find Kate, added as much information as he could about himself to his online page in the hope that Kate would find him.

Now that Kate had found Jane, it made her wonder whether she could find her old friend Mike.

Every sign that was shown to Kate kept coming back to one person: Mike. By then Kate had managed to become the observer of her own thoughts. She had learned to keep her mind clear so that she could hear the messages that the angels sent her. Kate knew that if she asked the angels to help her find Mike, they would surely make it happen—and they did. Mike had already updated his details on one of the main computer sites, and all she had to do was type in his name and his old city, and there he was.

While Fergus was watching how everything unfolded, he could not tell who was the most excited, Kate or Mike.

It didn't take the two of them very long to realise that they had been destined to meet again, and they knew their love was so strong that it would bind them together forever.

Chapter 14

Kate did not think her life could get any better than it already was. She was working with Kay, putting on workshops and talks to help people overcome the many problems that they had. Now Kate, Kay, and Mike worked together. There were three of them to share all the magic that was on their own planet and in the universe. They all had the same mission on earth: to create a better world for children.

Kate's long-term hope was that all children would be cared for in a whole new way. What she wanted was for all children and adults to know just how special they were, and that life did not have to be hard. The three of them wanted people to know how magical life can be, because then they would know who they really were.

When Kate became pregnant, she and Mike were over the moon. It was not something they had planned, but they were so happy to be given a special little child.

Kate already knew how to look after herself and her unborn baby inside of her. She used all-natural ingredients when she cooked, cleaned, and took care of her body. The one thing that she did more than anything was shower herself with as much love as possible. She knew that keeping calm would help keep her baby calm. She also knew that the love she gave to herself would be passed on to her child, helping him grow strong and helping his brain have the best chance to develop as much as possible.

Kate and Mike talked to their baby as much as they could while he was in her tummy. They knew that their baby would be familiar with their voices, so when it was time for him to be born, he would be comforted at hearing the loving voices of his parents.

Chapter 15

All that was left now for Abraham was to give Fergus some last-minute advice. He had helped Fergus as much as he could, but there were two things he still wanted Fergus to know.

Fergus knew the time for him to leave was coming close, and he was still a bit anxious. He had heard and seen his parents, and he believed that they would be good parents, but he did not feel as much love for them as he thought he would. Fergus believed if his heart was filled with love now, it would be even easier for him when he arrived on earth.

When Abraham appeared before Fergus, he could feel that his young student was nearly ready to leave. Abraham was so proud of Fergus; he was a delightful young soul, and the guide felt very protective towards him. These new souls had so much to give to the new world, and Abraham was pleased that there were now many adults ready to help them with their missions. Many children and young people who were already on earth had been called crystal and indigo children. These new children were now being called rainbow children. Abraham knew exactly what to tell him.

"Fergus, before you go, you already know that there will be people to help you everywhere, and all you have to do is follow the signs that we send you. There is one additional piece of information that I can tell you, and that is to watch out for the rainbows as they appear in the sky. Most people on earth love rainbows and are happy to point them out to children whenever they see them. Everyone believes that there is a pot of gold under the rainbow that can never be found, because every time you move, so does the rainbow—or so it appears. You need to remember that when people tell you about the pot of gold that lies at the bottom of a rainbow, it is not a pot of gold—it is you. Everything is you because you are connected to everything and everyone. The pot of gold represents finding your true self, so remember to keep looking out for the rainbows. You may also like to know that your mum's work name is Rainbow Keeper, so you can be assured that she will point out everything magical in life and help you find your way."

Abraham called his friend to come close to him. He wanted to show Fergus one last thing. It was a dream that Fergus's mother had had only the night before.

Fergus saw his mother standing and talking with two people, a man and a lady. Close to them were boats lined up in the water, and Kate could see families who were living on the boats and looked to be from another country. They had no food or shelter, and it was so cold outside. She had been asked to go there to meet two people, who wanted to ask her if she could help the refugees. In her dream Kate felt totally helpless, not knowing how she could make a difference to these children and their parents. She felt like she did not belong there. She could not speak their language, and she was worried that they would not accept her.

While Kate lay in bed dreaming, she saw herself walking away and shaking her head because she could not help them. Fergus understood this, but what he saw next turned his world upside down. He saw his mother the next day. She was crying and had been all day. Fergus felt so much love and compassion towards his mother that he felt like crying too. But it was not the end of the vision. When Kate told Mike about the dream, he simply wrapped his arms protectively around her and whispered, "We will do everything we can to make our planet a better place for all earth's children."

Abraham looked towards Fergus and smiled. He could see the love vibrating within the boy as he asked, "Are you ready, child?"

Fergus looked at his teacher and nodded, and with that he was gone.

Lightning Source UK Ltd.
Milton Keynes UK
UKOW04f0209190915

258816UK00001BA/5/P